The Ghost of Skip-Count Castle

by Spencer Brinker

Consultant:
Kimberly Brenneman, PhD
National Institute for Early Education Research
Rutgers University
New Brunswick, New Jersey

BEARPORT
PUBLISHING

New York, New York

Credits

Publisher: Kenn Goin
Editorial Director: Adam Siegel
Senior Editor: Joyce Tavolacci
Creative Director: Spencer Brinker
Photo Illustrations: Kim Jones

Library of Congress Cataloging-in-Publication Data

Brinker, Spencer, author.
  The ghost of Skip-Count Castle / by Spencer Brinker ; Consultant: Kimberly Brenneman,
PhD. National Institute for Early Education Research, Rutgers University, New Brunswick,
New Jersey.
      pages cm. — (Spooky math)
  Audience: Ages 4–8.
  Includes bibliographical references and index.
  ISBN-13: 978-1-62724-332-2 (library binding)
  ISBN-10: 1-62724-332-1 (library binding)
  1. Counting—Juvenile literature. 2. Ghosts—Juvenile literature. I. Title.
  QA113.B6873 2015
  513.2'11—dc23
                                                    2014012037

For more information, write to Bearport Publishing Company, Inc., 45 West 21st Street,
Suite 3B, New York, New York 10010. Printed in the United States of America.

10 9 8 7 6 5 4 3 2 1

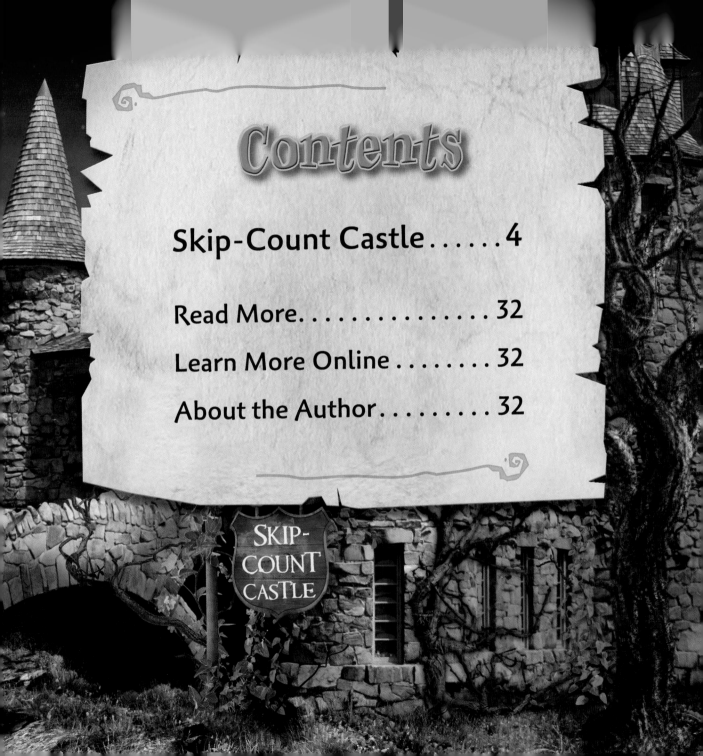

Contents

SKIP-
COUNT
CASTLE

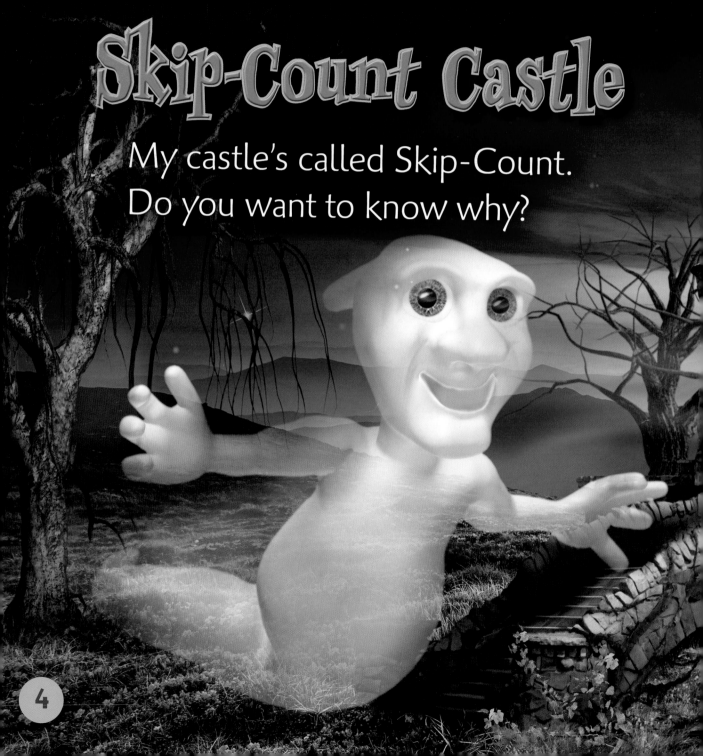

Skip-Count Castle

My castle's called Skip-Count.
Do you want to know why?

I'm a skip-counting ghost.
Come give it a try.

SKIP-
COUNT
CASTLE

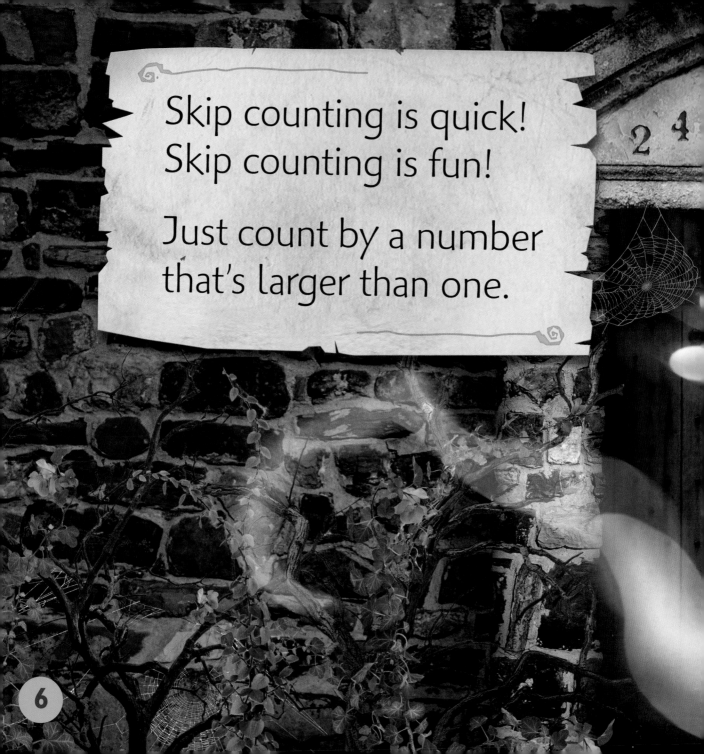

Skip counting is quick!
Skip counting is fun!

Just count by a number
that's larger than one.

SKIP-
COUNT
CASTLE

6 8 10

5 10 15 20 25

7

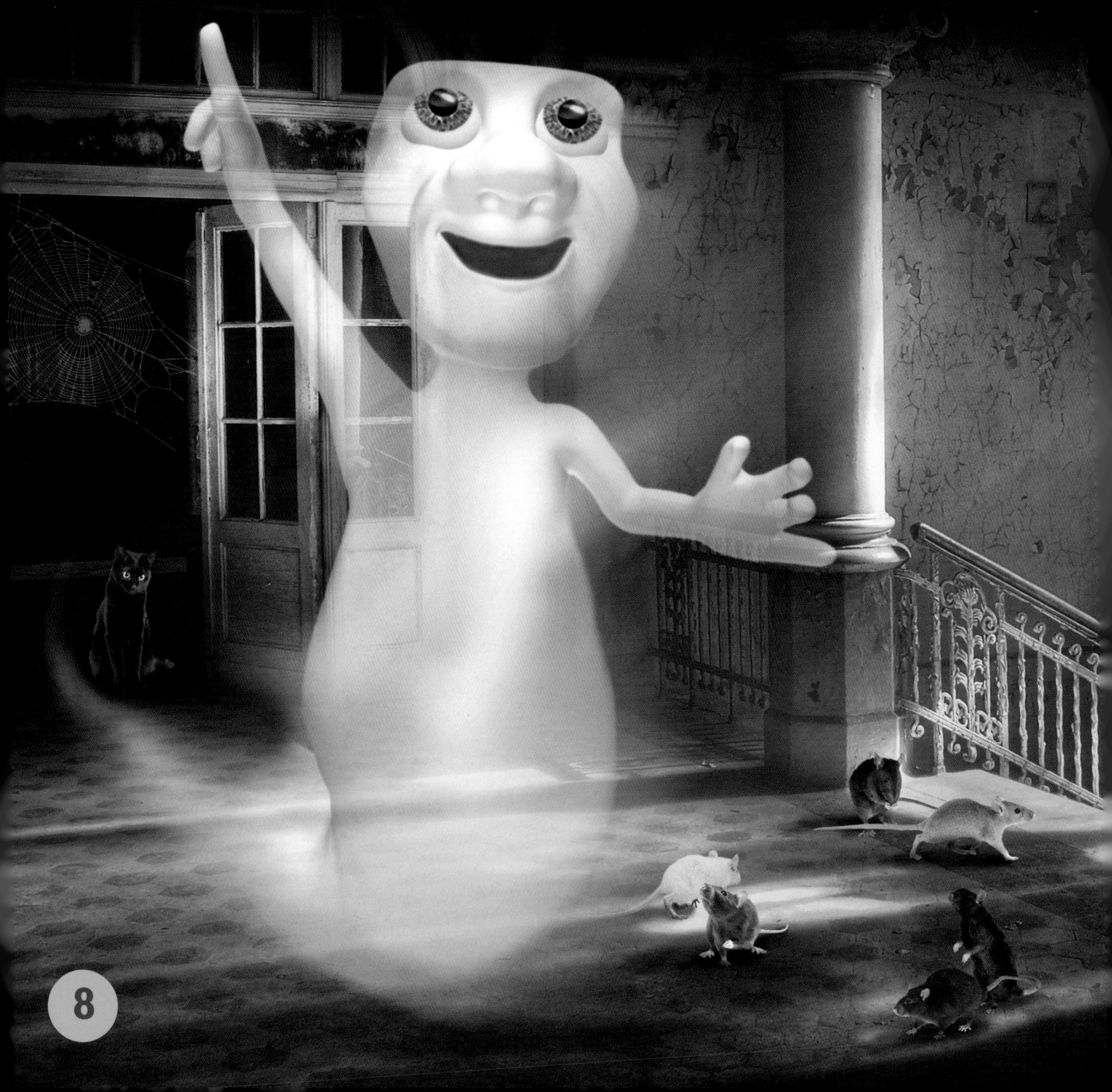

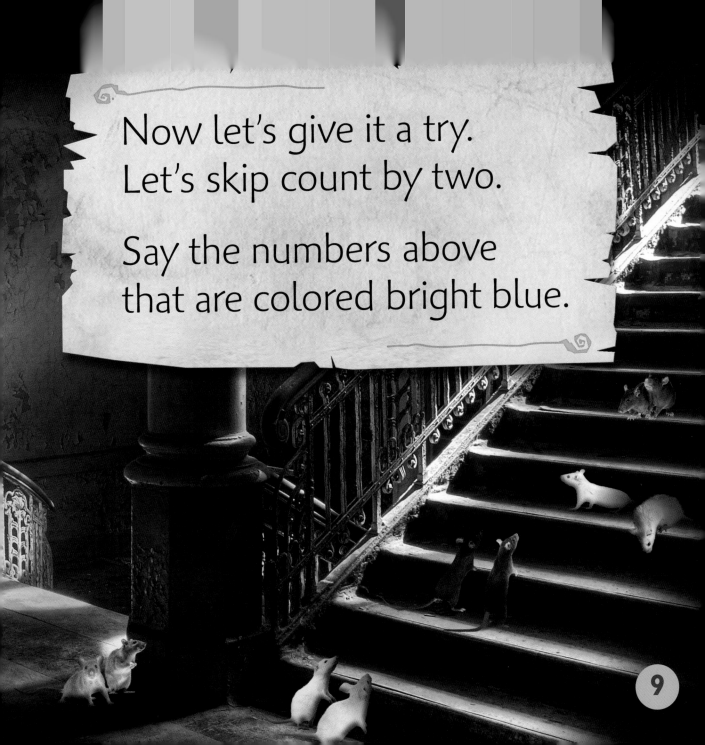

Now let's give it a try.
Let's skip count by two.

Say the numbers above
that are colored bright blue.

9

Some things come in pairs,
like basketball shoes.

To count them more quickly,
we count using twos.

My pals love to haunt.
So you'll hear many "Boos!"

How many ghosts are there?
Try counting by twos.

13

Can you spot all the eyes?
Just skip count by twos.

Which ones are most scary?
It's quite hard to choose.

Now let's move along,
and look in these big jars.

SEA STARS

Use fives to skip count
all the arms on these stars.

SEA STARS

Who's locked in this dungeon?
Well, nobody knows.

By twos, count their feet.
By fives, count their toes.

19

I've gathered these treasures
I got from my friends.

How many things are there?
Try counting by tens.

55 60 65 70 75 80 85 90 95 100

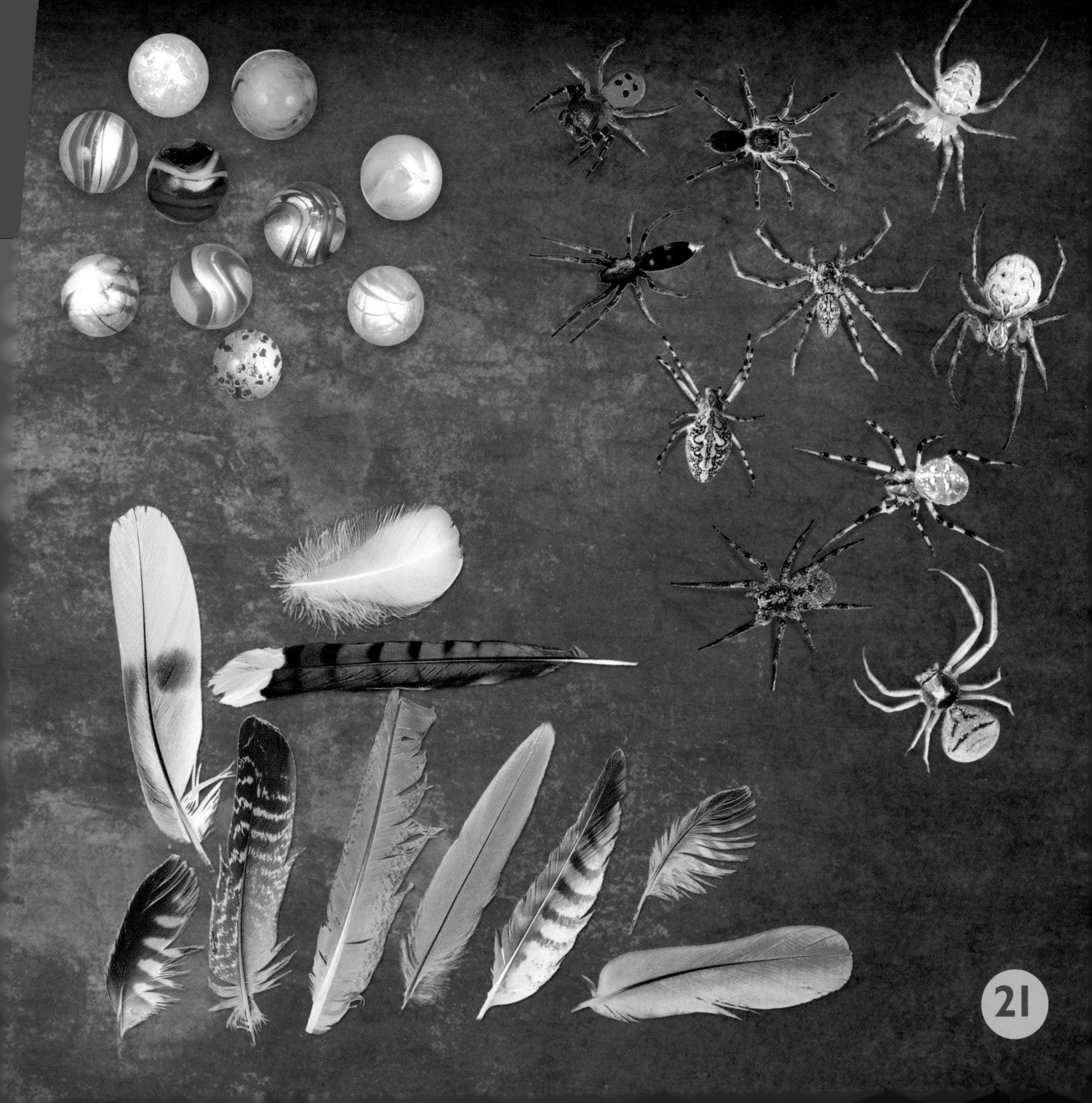

In each of these mouths
ten flower fangs fit.

22

Skip count the plants' teeth.
Try not to get bit!

23

5 10 15 20 25 30 35 40 45 50

Skip count by fives
the candles on the table.

24

Then count them again—
by tens if you're able.

What are wiggly and colorful?
The legs of these friends!

26

To skip count big numbers,
use fives or try tens.

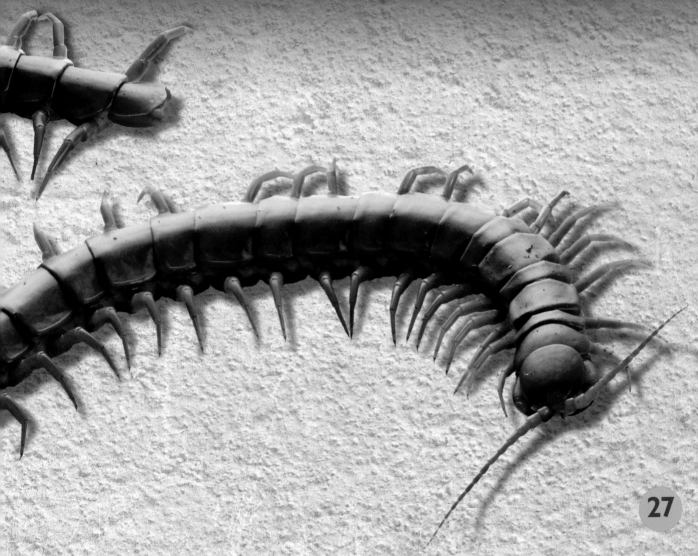

These beetles have spots.
There are ten on each back.

How many spots are there?
How many are black?

29

We've counted quite quickly
in such a fun way.

I'm glad you could join me
to skip count today.

Read More

Boothroyd, Jennifer.
*Skip Counting (First Step
Nonfiction)*. Minneapolis,
MN: Lerner (2007).

Steffora, Tracey. *Skip
Counting With Meerkats
(Animath)*. Chicago:
Heinemann (2014).

Learn More Online

To learn more about skip counting, visit
www.bearportpublishing.com/SpookyMath

About the Author

Spencer Brinker lives and works in New York
City. Having twin daughters helps him easily
skip count by twos.